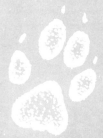

DESERT BABIES A–Z

RIO NUEVO PUBLISHERS®
P.O. Box 5250, Tucson, Arizona 85703-0250
(520) 623-9558, www.rionuevo.com

Design: Karen Schober, Seattle, Washington

Front cover: bobcat kitten; back cover: bighorn sheep; page 1: coyote pup; page 3: round-tailed ground squirrels.

Library of Congress Cataloging-in-Publication Data

Broyles, Bill.
  Desert babies A-Z / Bill Broyles ; photographs by Paul and Joyce Berquist.
    p. cm. -- (Look West)
  Includes index.
  ISBN 1-887896-69-4 (hardcover)
  1. Desert animals. I. Title. II. Series.
  QL116.B76 2005
  591.754--dc22

                        2004024556

Printed in Hong Kong
10 9 8 7 6 5 4 3 2 1

DESERT BABIES
A–Z

Bill Broyles

PHOTOGRAPHS BY **Paul and Joyce Berquist**

LOOK WEST
SERIES

TUCSON, ARIZONA

WE LOVE BABIES. CUTE, CUDDLY, AND SMALL,
THEY REMIND US OF OUR OWN CHILDHOODS: CRAWLING
AND TALKING, STANDING AND FALLING, LEARNING AND FAILING,
AND FINALLY SUCCEEDING AND GROWING UP. GANGLY, AWKWARD,
AND "FUNNY," THEY REMIND US OF BEING PARENTS AND
LOVINGLY CARING FOR YOUNG WHO EMBODY
OUR OWN CURIOSITY AND OPTIMISM.

In the desert and nearby mountains and riparian areas, from A (*Archilochus alexandri,* or black-chinned hummingbird) to Z (*Zenaida asiatica,* or white-winged dove), baby animals come in all shapes and sizes. Most desert babies are born in spring or after the summer rains, at times when plants—the foundation of the food chain—are

Bobcat kitten (opposite), baby ringtail (above).

lush with new leaves and flower nectar for babies or nursing mothers to eat. Insects, too, hatch in spring, providing food for cactus wrens, bats, and spiders. Hummingbirds nest in areas rich with flowers, which pump nectar and attract small insects, providing the mother with energy and a food supply to feed her chicks. Deer fawns hide in the new growth of grasses and shrubs, then learn to nibble shoots and tender leaves. Higher up the food chain, predators such as owls, coyotes, bobcats, and hawks take advantage of the boom in births to feed their own young.

White-tailed deer fawn.

As every parent knows, giving birth, feeding, and rearing young is tough work, so it's not surprising that animals have a variety of strategics to ensure that there is another generation of their species. Even giant desert centipedes guard their eggs and then their babies, letting them ride on mother's back. Wolf spiders and scorpions, too, protect their young until they can survive on their own.

Birds, on the other hand, lay and incubate eggs—but there's more to the story. Doves lay eggs on consecutive days, so squabs are born a day apart. This gives one of the babies a head start, and if food is scarce only the first chick may survive. Baby doves are born helpless, without feathers, and dumb as rocks. Parents must feed them until they leave the nest three weeks after hatching. Doves, roadrunners, thrashers, woodpeckers, cactus wrens, owls, and hawks are altricial, meaning their young are born helpless and dependent. Because the chicks demand so much care, these birds usually have no more than two to four babies at a time.

Altricial birds take care of their hatched chicks in nests hidden or camouflaged to blend in with the tree, thick grass, or ground. Parents also keep the nest clean and scent-free by removing body wastes and garbage. They put a winged roof over the youngsters, providing shade and shelter from sun and rain, as well as hiding the young from enemies. A hawk attacks any predators who approach its nest too closely, including people, while a dove may flee the nest, land on the ground, and pretend it has a broken wing so that the predator follows it away from the nest. Even tiny hummingbirds will take stabs at cats and roadrunners that threaten their nests.

Quail, on the other hand, are precocial birds, meaning the chicks are born ready to go. The eggs are laid on consecutive days, but the mother doesn't "sit" on them to begin the incubation period until the last one is laid, so the entire clutch hatches at the same time. Hatchlings are fuzzy with down and can already see and walk behind their parents. Because the chicks can feed themselves, precocial birds, including ducks, can have clutches of a dozen or more babies.

Many mammals—deer, pronghorns, coyotes, and foxes among them—deliver their babies in secluded, safe spots, where they nurse them for several weeks before taking them to join the herd or pack. The young "freeze" when anyone approaches the nest, and they generally have no scent and make no noise that might alert predators to where they are. These parents protect their young by chasing predators away, keeping the babies clean with tongue baths, and moving them from one den to another. Also, some parents may visit the den

Coyote pup.

only to bring food. Javelina babies and bighorn lambs, on the other hand, walk soon after birth and within a day or two join the herd, which protects them.

Most babies, be they birds or mammals, are drab and have tan or gray or spotted coats that blend in with the ground and surrounding vegetation. Bright colors—reds, yellows, blues—are reserved for adults trying to attract mates (not predators).

How do animal babies learn? Some knowledge is innate, born into the baby's brain and reactions. Baby lizards show no fear of bunnies, quail, or doves, but they instantly run or hide at the sight or shadow of a roadrunner, snake, or hawk. Animals that are not raised by parents must rely on innate knowledge and what they learn on their own, but experience is a hard teacher, so relatively few young live to be adults. From baby's perspective, there is much to know and many dangers to recognize. Every day is a test, and failure means becoming some other animal's meal.

But many animal parents do teach their young. Mountain lions, bobcats, coyotes, and foxes train their offspring to hunt, hide, find food, and stay out of trouble. Parents coach with nudges, growls, swats, nips, yips, whistles, and purrs. Quail chicks learn through imitation, following their parents as they scratch for seeds, bathe in dust, perch in trees at night, and fly by spreading their wings and jumping. The parents stay alert and call to the young when danger approaches, gathering the clutch of chicks and hiding them under outstretched wings or deep, covering leaves.

In my own yard in the Sonoran Desert, I watch newborn quail trail behind their parents, their little legs a blur as they try to keep up. I find it nearly impossible to count more than three quail chicks at a time as they swarm around their parents. Timid cottontails sneak up on a birdbath puddle for their first drink of water. Miniature spiny lizards, freshly hatched and small enough to curl back up inside a tiny egg, act like the biggest adults—they perch atop rocks, chase ants, do push-ups, and instinctively know to run and hide from a roadrunner on the prowl. Likely you, too, see animal babies in your own yard and neighborhood, wherever that may be.

Baby javelina.

BIGHORN SHEEP — *OVIS CANADENSIS*

SOFT-SOLED HOOVES CLING TO CLIFFS.

Rams gather harems of ewes during breeding season, and ewes form herds with lambs and yearlings the rest of the year. Lambs are born between February and April after 180 days of gestation. A mother will deliver her lamb in some secluded area safe from predators, then keep it hidden for a week until it is strong enough to walk. Young ewes and rams both begin to grow horns in a couple of months and are weaned at five to six months, but they remain with their mothers for up to two years.

Bighorns are excellent climbers; even lambs are amazingly agile and romp on slopes and near precipices that would give a human mother a nervous breakdown. They browse during daylight, especially early and late in the day, and bed down at night, though they may feed at night during bright phases of the moon. These ruminants eat a wide variety of plants, including ironwood leaves, mesquite beans, shrubs, flowers, grasses, and barrel cacti, from which they obtain moisture. Herds may include five to twenty animals.

The Rocky Mountain bighorn sheep is the state mammal of Colorado.

SPANISH	*borrego cimarrón*
HABITAT	Sonora, Mexico, to British Columbia, Canada; slopes of rugged mountains, including isolated desert ranges
PREDATORS	mountain lions, coyotes, bobcats, and humans
ADULT SIZE	rams stand 3–3½ feet at shoulder, 125–300 pounds; ewes stand 2½–3 feet, 75–200 pounds
LIFE EXPECTANCY	up to 15 years

BLACK-CHINNED HUMMINGBIRD ❧ *ARCHILOCHUS ALEXANDRI*

TINIEST BIRD IS FUELED BY NECTAR.

Black-chin courtship involves high, swooping aerobatics performed by the male to impress the female. After mating, the female lays two eggs in a small, camouflaged nest—hardly bigger than a thimble—made of spiderwebs, twigs, and leaf fragments. Incubation lasts thirteen to sixteen days. The mother feeds and cares for the babies alone, with usually only a single brood a year. Babies fledge in about three weeks and may remain with the mother for several days to weeks before setting off on their own.

Black-chinned hummingbirds have three types of territory: a breeding area that includes a nest, a mating area, and a male feeding area. Individuals defend these areas against other hummingbirds. Black-chins summer in the United States and winter in Mexico, migrating several thousand miles annually. Though solitary, they all tend to migrate at the same time. Black-chins visit a wide variety of flowers, especially ocotillo, chuparosa, honeysuckle, and wolfberry, relying on the sugar in flower nectar to satisfy their enormous energy requirements. Young and adults also eat small, soft-bodied insects and spiders for protein. They are very active during the day but become torpid at night, perching on small limbs to sleep and save their energy for the next day's constant activity.

SPANISH	*chuparrito garganti-negro, barbanegro, colibrí gorjinegro*
HABITAT	western United States and Mexico; woodlands, streamsides, mountain canyons, and cities
PREDATORS	cats, roadrunners, and king snakes
ADULT SIZE	3½ inches, 3–4 grams
LIFE EXPECTANCY	several years

BLACK-TAILED JACKRABBIT ⬩ *LEPUS CALIFORNICUS*
RADIATOR EARS AND TWENTY-FOOT LEAPS.

This hare, unlike a true rabbit such as the desert cottontail, is born ready to go. Mating may occur in any month, and parents may have as many as four litters a year, of two to four babies each, after forty-three days of gestation. Newborns have hair, can see, and can walk. The mother hides them in small nests and nurses them at night. They are weaned at twelve to thirteen weeks and mature after one year.

These jackrabbits may feed in groups and are tolerant of others, except for males competing for females. Preferred fare includes grasses, leaves and bark, mesquite beans, and cacti. Jacks have keen hearing and eyesight, and their exceptionally large ears allow their blood to cool on hot days, helping them to handle summer heat.

They are most active at night, dawn, and dusk. During midday they rest under small bushes at any of several comfortable "forms" (or depressions) they dig for themselves. Forms are usually shaded by plants or rocks and provide shelter from full sun, rain, or predators.

Jackrabbits usually hop instead of walk to food supplies, up to a couple of miles away. When frightened, they may escape at thirty-five miles an hour for up to half a mile, zigzagging in a series of twenty-foot leaps. Every

fourth or fifth hop may be higher than the others so the jack can better view the predator or terrain. They can swim but seldom have the opportunity.

SPANISH	*liebre*
HABITAT	western United States; open and semi-open areas such as meadows, valleys, prairies, and creosote-bush flats
PREDATORS	coyotes, owls, hawks, large snakes, and foxes
ADULT SIZE	body 1½–2 feet tall, 4–8 pounds
LIFE EXPECTANCY	up to 7 years

BLACK-TAILED PRAIRIE DOG ⌐ *CYNOMYS LUDOVICIANUS*
DOG TOWNS AND COMMUNITY SPIRIT.

Prairie dogs spend their days near their prairie dog "towns," feeding on roots and grasses, and occasionally on insects such as grasshoppers. They seldom stray far from an entrance to the village for safety reasons. A communal maze of rooms, entrances, and tunnels may cover hundreds of acres and accommodate thousands of individuals. Tunnels are "engineered" to provide ventilation and may extend fifteen feet below the surface. Dirt from the tunnels is mounded

around the entrances. Members are very vocal and very social, making whistled warnings when a predator approaches, and they groom each other. In winter the "dogs" sleep a lot but do not truly hibernate.

Families usually consist of one male, one to four females, and their offspring up to two years of age. Mating occurs in February, with four to five young born in March or April, and babies first appear aboveground in May.

SPANISH	*perro-llanero cola negra, perro de la pradera de cola negra*
HABITAT	New Mexico to Montana; prairies and grasslands; soft, deep soil
PREDATORS	hawks, eagles, snakes, badgers, coyotes, foxes, and ferrets
ADULT SIZE	14–16 inches long including tail, 2–3 pounds
LIFE EXPECTANCY	7–8 years

BOBCAT *FELIS RUFUS*

NAMED FOR ITS SHORT "BOBBED" TAIL.

Kittens are born in late spring, usually in litters of two to three, and stay with their mother until fall, while she teaches them to hunt. Bobcats prefer to eat rabbits, mice, snakes, birds, lizards, and small deer. They usually hunt by stalking or by lying in ambush. Bobcats are solitary, except for mothers with kittens. They locate their dens in thick vegetation, under ledges, in small caves, and under houses. Like most cats, they are excellent climbers and can also swim.

SPANISH *gato montés*

HABITAT throughout the United States, including deserts; rugged, thickly vegetated, rocky areas and along washes—surprisingly common in suburban areas that have wooded or brushy spaces

PREDATORS mountain lions, coyotes, other bobcats, bears, and humans

ADULT SIZE body 2–3 feet long, 14–22 pounds

LIFE EXPECTANCY up to 7 years in the wild, longer in captivity

CACTUS WREN ⋈ *CAMPYLORHYNCHUS BRUNNEICAPILLUS*

BUILDS DECOY NESTS AND IS WARY OF INTRUDERS—EVEN CARS.

Cactus wrens build several nests—hollow globes of sticks and grass, with odds and ends such as feathers of other birds, often built in

protective cactus plants—and select one in which to raise young. In March, three to five eggs are laid, requiring sixteen days of incubation. Both parents help rear the young, bringing them small insects four to seven times an hour until they fledge after three weeks. Then the chicks beg from and follow their parents for several weeks until they set off on their own. Parents may raise one to three broods annually. These wrens feed on spiders, insects, fruit pulp, and occasionally seeds.

The cactus wren is Arizona's state bird.

SPANISH	*matraca desértica, matraca grande*
HABITAT	Southwest deserts, arid foothills; cactus forests, mesquite trees, yuccas, and shrubs
PREDATORS	climbing snakes, cats, owls, rodents, and roadrunners
ADULT SIZE	7–8½ inches, 1½ ounces
LIFE EXPECTANCY	4 years or more

CAROLINA WOLF SPIDER ⋖ *HOGNA CAROLINENSIS*
A SPIDER THAT WALKS ON WATER!

The mother wolf spider carries her egg cases with her, sometimes sunning them to hasten hatching. In a month the eggs are ready, and she bites a hole in the case, releasing as many as one hundred spiderlings. Sustained by yolk from their eggs, the spiderlings live on their mother's back for a week before wandering off to lead their own lives. Wolf spiders are solitary and live in burrows that can be identified by a spider-silk rim camouflaged and reinforced with bits of plants. They hunt roaches, beetles, other spiders, and moths at night and can walk on water when hunting on small ponds.

SPANISH	*buena madre, carga hijas, mordelena*
HABITAT	throughout the United States from deserts to woodlands
PREDATORS	bats, other spiders, and lizards
ADULT SIZE	body 1 inch long, legs 1–1½ inches
LIFE EXPECTANCY	2 years

COUCH'S SPADEFOOT TOAD *SCAPHIOPUS COUCHI*

DIGS WITH "SPADES" AND HAS THUNDEROUS ALARM CLOCK.

These are not true toads—they lack parotoid glands but have vertical pupils, relatively smooth skin, teeth in the upper jaw, and a coccyx fused to the sacral vertebra—so it's okay to call them spadefoots. Adults mate in pools after heavy summer rains, then females may lay as many as three thousand eggs, which can hatch within thirty-six hours in a race to develop before the pool dries. Tadpoles grow legs and can survive out of water as soon as ten days after hatching, but they can take up to a month if the pool holds water. Individuals leave the pools to feed on nocturnal insects and to burrow in soft soil as deep as six feet by using the spade-horns on their rear feet to dig. They are active in summer and can hibernate for many months during dry times, until thunder or pounding rain awakens them.

Spadefoots eat beetles, grasshoppers, spiders, ants, and termites, and may eat enough in one evening's feast to sustain them through the next year. Spadefoots secrete an irritant that repels some predators. This common desert dweller bleats like a lamb and can be heard up to a mile away.

SPANISH	*sapo con espuelas*
HABITAT	western Texas to southern Arizona; dry arroyos, grasslands, mesquite and creosote flats, stock tanks, and clay and gravel flats
PREDATORS	tadpoles are eaten by birds, dragonfly larvae, and even other cannibalistic tadpoles; toads are eaten by snakes, birds, and some mammals
ADULT SIZE	2½–3½ inches long, ½–3 ounces
LIFE EXPECTANCY	several years

COYOTE ⚜ *CANIS LATRANS*

"SONGDOGS" SING IN CITIES TOO.

Coyotes are social animals, and packs may include up to a dozen members of varying ages. Pups are born in dens—usually burrows or small caves—after two months of gestation. Mothers have one litter

a year, averaging five pups, who leave the den after nine to ten weeks to travel and hunt with adults. Opportunistic feeders, coyotes may hunt as a pack and will eat almost anything, including rodents, rabbits, berries, cactus fruit, snakes, birds, carrion, fish, and grass.

Coyotes can run up to thirty miles an hour and cover long distances at a slower, more efficient dogtrot. They can also swim. Adults may travel four hundred miles from their birthplace. Their scientific name means "barking dog," and their wide variety of memorable howls, yips, and barks have come to symbolize the Wild West.

SPANISH   *coyote*

HABITAT   throughout North America except the Arctic; valleys, plains, grasslands, deserts, and lower mountains—very adaptable, some live in suburbs and even in cities where they can find food, shelter, and open space such as golf courses and arroyo banks

PREDATORS   mountain lions, bobcats, bears, and humans

ADULT SIZE   23–26 inches at the shoulder, 20–40 pounds

LIFE EXPECTANCY   up to 14 years

DESERT TORTOISE ∻ *GOPHERUS AGASSIZII*

THE DESERT'S ELDER STATESMAN.

Mating may occur throughout the summer, although females wait to dig their nests and lay clutches of one to fifteen eggs each, early in

the following summer. Eggs generally hatch in ninety days but may take longer if the weather is cooler. Tortoises in the Mojave Desert may lay one to three clutches per year, but those in the Sonoran Desert lay just one clutch. Hatchlings have soft shells, receive no parental care, and take fifteen years to reach maturity.

Tortoises are solitary except when mating or denning for winter hibernation or summer aestivation, when they hide in small rock shelters or dig burrows. In warmer months, they hide from predators and sleep under plants, rocks, and wood-rat nests as they move around their home territory. They feed on a wide variety of plants in daytime. If they have water to drink, they can eat dried plants. Otherwise, they require moist, green plants, including succulents and cactus fruit.

The desert tortoise is California's state reptile.

SPANISH	*tortuga del desierto*
HABITAT	Sonoran and Mojave Deserts; rocky foothills, desert valleys
PREDATORS	young tortoises are eaten by ravens, coyotes, and snakes
ADULT SIZE	10–14 inches long, 5–8 pounds
LIFE EXPECTANCY	40 years or more

ELF OWL ⊰ *MICRATHENE WHITNEYI* ‖
THE LITTLEST OWL, TINY AS AN ELF.

In early spring, elf owls migrate northward to feed on emerging insects. Parents nest in woodpecker holes in saguaro cacti and old trees. A clutch of three to four eggs is incubated for twenty-one to twenty-four days, and the young fledge in four weeks, able to catch crickets on their own, but they may stay with the parents several more weeks. Both parents help rear the owlets. Elf owls feed on insects (crickets, moths, beetles, grasshoppers) and arachnids (spiders and even scorpions, though they remove the stingers first). This is the smallest owl in America.

SPANISH	*tecolote enano*
HABITAT	eastern California to central Mexico, including southern Arizona; saguaro forests, wooded canyons, and desert shrublands
PREDATORS	snakes, foxes, other owls, and hawks
ADULT SIZE	5–6 inches tall, 1½ ounces
LIFE EXPECTANCY	several years

GAMBEL'S QUAIL ≼ *CALLIPEPLA GAMBELII*

NUMBER OF CHICKS DEPENDS ON WINTER RAIN.

Gambel's quail mate in spring and usually have only one brood per year. The hen lays ten to twenty eggs in a concealed nest on the ground and incubates them for twenty-one to twenty-four days. Chicks all hatch on the same day and are precocial, able to walk within a few hours. The down-covered young follow and imitate their very protective parents as they scratch for seeds and catch small

insects, and the family stays together for most of the first year. Although quail eat mainly seeds, they derive vitamins from flowers and leafy plants, and protein from insects. They form coveys of twenty to fifty birds in the fall, pairing off again in spring.

SPANISH	*codorniz de Gambel*
HABITAT	southwestern United States; desert thickets and flats
PREDATORS	hawks, snakes, roadrunners, bobcats, foxes, coyotes, and humans; their eggs are a favorite food of Gila monsters and gopher snakes
ADULT SIZE	10–11½ inches long, 6 ounces
LIFE EXPECTANCY	several years

GRAY FOX ⊰ *UROCYON CINEREOARGENTEUS*
THE ONLY CANINE THAT CLIMBS TREES.

An excellent climber, the gray fox sometimes hunts in trees and may even sleep in trees—even on the arm of a saguaro. Foxes hunt and forage by day, choosing from a wide menu of rodents, birds, rabbits, berries, grasses, and fruits. Gray foxes breed in late winter, and pups arrive after a gestation of fifty-one to sixty-three days. Like other canines, they are helpless when born. Weaned at six weeks, they learn to hunt from both parents within four months after birth.

SPANISH *zorro gris*

HABITAT eastern, midwestern, southern, and far western United States; rocky and brushy areas, woodlands, open desert; dens in rock crevices, boulder piles, hollow logs, and sometimes in badger burrows

PREDATORS coyotes, bobcats, feral dogs, and humans

ADULT SIZE 14–15 inches tall at shoulder, 7–13 pounds

LIFE EXPECTANCY up to 13 years

GREAT HORNED OWL   *BUBO VIRGINIANUS*
CATCHES 1,000 MICE A YEAR.

In late winter this largest of owls lays two to three eggs in a nest made by a hawk or raven in a tree or on a flat ledge of a cliff or building. Incubation lasts thirty to thirty-five days. The owlets stay in the nest for five to seven weeks and are fed small mammals and birds. Young owls spend two to three weeks mastering flight, then stay with the parents until fall or early winter, learning to hunt and enjoying their protection.

The great horned owl has extremely acute hearing and keen night vision, and its soft feathers allow it to hunt silently. When the growing young are hungriest, parents also may hunt during the day.

They prefer to eat rabbits and rodents, but will take birds, lizards, insects, frogs, and fish. On still desert nights, the hoot of this owl—as distinctive as the howl of a coyote—can be heard a mile away.

SPANISH	*buho, tecolote cornudo*
HABITAT	throughout North America except the Arctic; deserts to forests to prairies and grasslands
PREDATORS	has few enemies
ADULT SIZE	22–25 inches tall, 3 pounds
LIFE EXPECTANCY	up to 27 years

HARRIS'S HAWK ❧ *PARABUTEO UNICINCTUS*
HUNTING IS A FAMILY AFFAIR.

Harris's hawks build platform nests of sticks in trees between February and June. Usually two to three eggs are laid in late spring, and incubation takes twenty-nine to thirty-five days. The young fledge in forty to forty-five days but may remain with the family for up to four years, learning to hunt and helping rear the next generations of chicks. Typical breeding groups include up to seven birds—at least one dominant adult female, two adult males, and several immature males or females—that work together hunting to feed the young.

Social birds, Harris's hawks hunt together in the daytime, allowing them to take larger prey and more prey per hour, with less risk of injury. They take rodents such as ground squirrels and wood rats, birds on the ground, rabbits, lizards, and even big insects. For some reason, they decline to eat snakes.

SPANISH	*águila cinchada*
HABITAT	southern Arizona and Texas to Central America; mesquite scrublands, woodlands, and saguaro desert
PREDATORS	they have few enemies but are sometimes harassed by kestrels, ravens, and other hawks
ADULT SIZE	20 inches tall, 2 pounds
LIFE EXPECTANCY	several years

HOODED SKUNK ⚔ *MEPHITIS MACROURA*
STRIPED SKUNK ⚔ *MEPHITIS MEPHITIS*

YOU CAN SMELL US FOR A MILE.

Skunks eat almost anything, including insects, grubs, eggs, frogs, small mammals, lizards, snakes, carrion, seeds, and fruit. They are nocturnal and spend their days in dens made in small caves, thickets, burrows, and under buildings in suburbia. Skunks defend

Striped skunk

Hooded skunk

themselves by spraying a very foul-smelling, musky liquid ten to fifteen feet; discomfort from the mist (nausea, burning eyes and nose) may reach three times that far, and the odor may be detected as far as a mile away. Fortunately they are slow to anger and usually stomp their feet or give warning before the memorable barrage. They are hunted by great horned owls, which seem immune to the smell.

Mating occurs from February to April, and after gestation of fifty-nine to seventy-seven days, litters of four to five kits are born. They are weaned at eight to ten weeks but follow their mother until they mature at about a year of age.

SPANISH *zorillo* (hooded skunk); *zorillo listado* (striped skunk)

HABITAT Southwest borderland (hooded skunk); throughout United States (striped skunk); foothills, brushy areas, woodlands, deserts, and thickets along streams

PREDATORS great horned owls

ADULT SIZE 20–30 inches long, 6–14 pounds

LIFE EXPECTANCY 6–12 years

JAVELINA · *PECARI TAJACU*

REPEAT AFTER ME: I AM NOT A PIG; I'M A PECCARY.

Mating usually occurs in February and March, with young born during summer after a gestation of 115 days. Their birth coincides with summer rains greening up a variety of plants. Born in thickets, rock caves, or burrows dug by other animals, the newborns—usually twins—have a reddish brown coat and are called "reds." They can walk within a few hours and join the herd the next day, escorted by their mother. The herd, led by an elder sow, is very protective. Reds nurse six to eight weeks and mature in a year.

Javelinas frequently clean themselves, taking dust and mud baths, but they still exude a musky smell that enables members of a herd to identify each other. Their eyesight is poor, so they may appear to charge at people when spooked, when they are actually trying to escape. They can gallop up to twenty-five miles an hour and can swim if they need to.

Some predators occasionally try to eat javelinas, especially young ones, but their speed, agility, and formidable teeth offer good defense. Humans also hunt them. In summer they tend to be nocturnal to avoid the heat, but in winter they forage by day. Herds may include up to fifty animals, with most groups numbering five to fifteen. They prefer prickly pear cactus fruits, pads, and roots but will eat a wide variety of leaves, beans, berries, nuts, and roots. Sometimes they eat snakes, frogs, rodents, or carrion. They do not seem to be affected by rattlesnake bites.

SPANISH	*jabalí*
HABITAT	southwestern United States to South America; in deserts, low mountains, valleys, and woodlands where there are prickly pear cacti
PREDATORS	mountain lions, bobcats, coyotes, and humans
ADULT SIZE	stands 20–24 inches tall, 40–55 pounds
LIFE EXPECTANCY	up to 24 years

MOUNTAIN LION ≋ *FELIS CONCOLOR*

WIDE-RANGING NAVIGATORS.

Litters of one to six kittens are born about ninety-six days after mating, which may occur any time of the year, and the young remain with their mother for up to two years while she protects them and teaches them to hunt. Mothers can purr and have a number of calls and commands, perhaps including some that humans cannot hear. Adults are solitary except for brief mating periods and mothers with offspring.

To establish their own territories, young toms move an average of sixty miles from where they were born. Females establish territories next to their mother's range. They are very faithful to their home ranges, and documented cases show lions being "blindfolded," released four hundred miles from home, and finding their way back over unknown terrain within six months. They are good climbers and swimmers. Generally lions shun humans and seldom are seen. By day they rest in thickets, small caves, and sheltered rocky areas.

Although they prefer deer, lions will eat rabbits, javelinas, mice, birds, coyotes, and other mountain lions. For short distances they can outrun deer, though they generally hunt from ambush or by stalking

and then pouncing on their prey. Adults may cover twenty-five miles a night while hunting and need only one deer a week to feed on.

SPANISH	*puma, león de la sierra*
HABITAT	from Alaska to Tierra del Fuego (largest range of any mammal in Northern Hemisphere); forests of both mountains and deserts—prefers very wild, big places
PREDATORS	other lions and humans; kittens are vulnerable to coyotes, bobcats, and bears
ADULT SIZE	6 feet long, 75–150 pounds
LIFE EXPECTANCY	up to 15 years

MULE DEER ⊰ *ODOCOILEUS HEMIONUS*
WHITE-TAILED DEER ⊰ *ODOCOILEUS VIRGINIANUS*

ANTLERS GROW AT RECORD SPEED.

Most of the year, female deer, or does, form herds with fawns and yearlings, while bucks live alone or in small groups. Breeding takes place in winter, and fawns—often twins—are born in summer, after a gestation of seven months. Their spotted coats help camouflage them, and they lie quietly in secluded beds for two to four weeks, until able to walk with the herd. By the age of two months the spots disappear. Mothers nurse their fawns every four hours, but by two weeks of age the young can also nibble green plants. They mature in a year to eighteen months.

When spooked, mule deer may run or bound away stiff-legged, as if on pogo sticks, while white-tailed deer flash their white tails to warn the herd and then run. Deer are adept at hiding and at moving without being seen. They are capable swimmers and can run short distances at thirty-five miles an hour.

Deer browse on a variety of shrubs and trees, including sagebrush, cliff rose, aspen, juniper, oak leaves and acorns, mesquite beans and leaves, and jojoba, and they occasionally graze on forbs and grasses. White-tailed deer require drinking water, but mule deer may survive on moisture found in plants. Deer are active during mornings, evenings, and moonlit nights. By day they bed down in shaded, sheltered areas under trees or in thickets. Bucks drop their antlers in February but regrow them by September.

SPANISH	*venado burro* (mule deer), *venado cola blanca* (white-tailed deer)
HABITAT	western United States (mule deer); throughout the United States (white-tailed deer)
PREDATORS	mountain lions, bears, coyotes, and humans
ADULT SIZE	mule deer: 3–3½ feet tall, 110–400 pounds; white-tailed deer: 3–3½ feet tall, 90–300 pounds
LIFE EXPECTANCY	up to 10 years

White-tailed deer.

REGAL HORNED LIZARD ≼ *PHRYNOSOMA SOLARE*
EYES SQUIRT BLOOD TO SPOOK PREDATORS.

Ants compose about 90 percent of this horned lizard's diet. They are immune to the irritant in ant stings but may suffer from their nipping bites. These solitary lizards burrow underground in sand to escape predators and intense sun, and hibernate in winter. Horned lizards are pursued by a variety of predators, although the spiny "collars" on the adults make them difficult to swallow. They also squirt blood from their eyes to deter coyotes and foxes. Their coloration and flat shape allow them to hide by blending in with the ground.

In midsummer, regal horned lizards lay an average of twenty-one eggs in carefully selected nests. The babies hatch in five to nine weeks, but parents do not care for their young; the few that survive to adulthood mature in their second year.

The related Texas horned lizard is Texas's state reptile.

SPANISH	*camaleón*
HABITAT	southern Arizona and Sonora, Mexico; arid and semiarid flats and valleys; prefers gravelly, rocky, sandy slopes
PREDATORS	snakes, lizards, and birds such as the roadrunner
ADULT SIZE	$2\frac{1}{2}$–$4\frac{1}{2}$ inches long
LIFE EXPECTANCY	up to 8 years

RINGTAIL ⚔ *BASSARISCUS ASTUTUS*

RACCOON RELATIVE IS NATURE'S GYMNAST.

Large eyes enable ringtails to forage at night for rodents, birds, lizards, fruit, and insects. Ringtails are superb climbers, using their tails for balance. Their rear feet can rotate 180 degrees, so they can walk down precipices and ropes as well as climb them. By day they hide in crevices, small caves, and hollow trees. They will even live in the attics of people's cabins, which led frontiersmen to call them "miner's cats." Though seldom seen, their rustling may be heard at night or their odor smelled near dens. Ringtails mate in April, bearing two to four young after a pregnancy of fifty-one to fifty-four days. Both parents may care for the babies, which forage with the parents by two months of age and are weaned by four months. Ringtails mature at ten months and are solitary for much of the year.

The ringtail is Arizona's state mammal.

SPANISH	*cacomixtle, cacomistle*
HABITAT	southwestern United States; rocky areas of mountains, usually near water
PREDATORS	owls, bobcats, and coyotes
ADULT SIZE	24–30 inches long, 1½–2½ pounds
LIFE EXPECTANCY	up to 14 years

ROUND-TAILED GROUND SQUIRREL
SPERMOPHILUS TERETICAUDUS

SEED LOVERS WITH UNDERGROUND APARTMENTS.

Round-tailed ground squirrels mate in March and April, and after twenty-seven days, two to eight blind, hairless babies are born. Litters are smaller in dry years and larger in wet years. The young are weaned at four to six weeks and reach maturity at eleven months.

They eat seeds, buds, beans, leafy plants, cactus pulp and fruit, and occasionally carrion, climbing trees and cacti to find food. Round-tails are active during the day, but in summer they rest in shade or in their burrows during the hottest hours. In winter they hibernate. These gregarious squirrels dig extensive systems of communal tunnels, with rooms used for sleeping, birthing, and perhaps seed storage. The tunnels have several entrances—or exits, if a snake enters. Predation prevents most from attaining old age.

SPANISH	*juancito*
HABITAT	creosote-bush and saltbush deserts of Arizona and California; desert flatlands and valleys; sandy or loose soil
PREDATORS	hawks, roadrunners, snakes, badgers, foxes, coyotes, and bobcats
ADULT SIZE	8–10 inches long including tail, 5–7 ounces
LIFE EXPECTANCY	up to 8 years

STRIPED-TAIL SCORPION ◄ *VEJOVIS SPINIGERUS*
400 MILLION YEARS OLD AND COUNTING.

Up to several dozen young are born at a time. Newborn scorpions live on their mother's back for several weeks while she guards them and shares food. They molt several times and mature in one to two years.

Scorpions are found on six continents, and fossils show that they have existed for at least 400 million years. They sting their prey and, in self-defense, predators. They excel at controlling insect pests such as roaches, crickets, and beetles. They can see clearly for only a few inches but can see in very dim light and are extremely sensitive to vibrations, smells, and light. Scorpions fluoresce and can be detected with a black light at night. They are masters of conserving moisture and energy, able to live in very hot, dry places. Scorpions are shy, secretive, and solitary.

SPANISH	*alacrán*
HABITAT	arid areas of the Southwest; hides under rocks, in thin crevices, or in subterranean, sandy burrows by day and hunts by night
PREDATORS	mice, owls, spiders, lizards, bats, and other scorpions
ADULT SIZE	2 inches long
LIFE EXPECTANCY	10 years or more

WESTERN DIAMONDBACK RATTLESNAKE
CROTALUS ATROX

DON'T FOOL WITH THESE NEWBORNS!

Baby diamondbacks are born alive in summer, with four to twenty-five in a brood. Starting out at eight to thirteen inches long, the

babies resemble adults and are independent at birth, which is timed to coincide with high rodent populations.

Diamondbacks are active except during the warmest parts of the day. Heat sensors and keen smell allow them to hunt at night, detecting recent animal trails and lying coiled in wait for prey to pass by. Their bite injects lethal poison, both to subdue the victim and to begin the process of digestion, before they swallow the victim whole. They eat rodents, rabbits, birds, and lizards.

Babies are born fully able to defend themselves with a venomous bite and to take small rodents and lizards. Newborns cannot rattle until they have grown big enough to shed their skin the first time. Adults generally buzz their tails to warn predators and people to stay away, although they may strike without buzzing. Solitary individuals gather to mate or to den during winter.

SPANISH	*víbora de cascabel*
HABITAT	throughout the southwestern United States from Oklahoma to California; prefer brushy, rocky canyons and foothills in arid and semiarid plains and mountains
PREDATORS	coyotes, hawks, owls, and king snakes
ADULT SIZE	3–7 feet, 1–4 pounds
LIFE EXPECTANCY	up to 26 years

WHITE-WINGED DOVE ~ *ZENAIDA ASIATICA*
ASKS "WHO COOKS FOR YOU?"

After mating, mothers lay two eggs in flimsy stick nests in low trees or tall cacti. The male sits on the nest during midday, and the female takes over from midafternoon through midmorning of the next day during thirteen to nineteen days of incubation. The squabs thrive on a diet of "pigeon milk"—a nutritious mixture of partially digested seeds and secretions of the parents' crops. Young pigeons fledge in sixteen days and are independent, though they may feed with parents and flocks.

Doves eat seeds and fruit, especially of giant saguaro cacti. Like lesser long-nosed bats, white-wings are instrumental in pollinating saguaros and dispersing their seeds. By early September most white-wings migrate south for the winter and return by mid-April.

SPANISH	*paloma aliblanca*
HABITAT	Southwest borderlands of Arizona and Texas to South America; saguaro desert, streamsides, mesquite and salt cedar thickets—and urban areas
PREDATORS	hawks, bobcats, large snakes, owls, and grackles
ADULT SIZE	11½ inches long, 5 ounces
LIFE EXPECTANCY	up to 15 years

BASIC READING

Behler, John L., and F. Wayne King. *The Audubon Society Field Guide to North American Reptiles and Amphibians.* New York: Alfred A. Knopf, 1989.

Hoffmeister, Donald F. *Mammals of Arizona.* Tucson, Arizona: University of Arizona Press and Arizona Game and Fish Department, 1986.

Nowak, Ronald M., and John L. Paradiso. *Walker's Mammals of the World.* 4th ed. Baltimore, Maryland: Johns Hopkins University Press, 1983.

Phillips, Steven M., and Patricia Wentworth Cormus. *A Natural History of the Sonoran Desert.* Tucson, Arizona: Arizona-Sonora Desert Museum Press, and Berkeley, California: University of California Press, 2000.

Sibley, David Allen. *The Sibley Guide to Bird Life and Behavior.* New York: Alfred A. Knopf, 2001.

Uvardy, Miklos D. F. *The Audubon Society Field Guide to North American Birds, Western Region.* New York: Alfred A. Knopf, 1990.

Whitaker, John O., Jr. *The Audubon Society Field Guide to North American Mammals.* New York: Alfred A. Knopf, 1993.

Baby rock squirrel.

INDEX